Words in the Flow

TAMMY CHEUNG

Copyright © 2022 Tammy Cheung

All rights reserved.

ISBN: 9781399939256

*To all those whom I have crossed path with
Who left pieces of their stories with me*

PREFACE

As a former Psychology major, I am intrigued by the concept of "flow" - a mental state in which you are completely immersed in what you are doing, giving you immense satisfaction and enjoyment.

Writing is one activity that gets me in the flow. One of the first poems I've written was a school assignment. After talking about Shakespeare and his sonnets, our teacher invited us to write our own love poems. Wanting my piece to differ from typical, sappy romantic verses, I wrote about how love had stayed with a girl since the beginning; on the smiles of her family around the cradle, between the guitar chords in the serenade strummed by a young boy, in the humble cottage she shared with her partner, and in the flowers around her tombstone.

Regrettably, I can't recall the entire content of the poem. As it is with many things, it was swept away down the river of life.

Roman emperor and Stoic philosopher, Marcus Aurelius, once wrote:

"Time is a sort of river of passing events, and strong is its current; no sooner is a thing brought to sight than it is swept by and another takes its place, and this too will be swept away."

Apparently, this was the forerunner of the common expression - "go with the flow". Some say Marcus Aurelius is implying one should accept things as they are and let life carry you along, while others read deeper into the meaning - that it is not wise to cling onto the way things are because change is relentless.

In my own words, here is how I aspire to "go with the flow":

Going with the flow is not slacking off
It's being mindful of when to let go
Sometimes when the waters get rough
You let it take you where it flows

In life you don't really need labels
But just experience it as it goes
While you go with the flow so they let you in
Note to also be at peace with your flow within.

Of course, it's not always easy. Countless people drift with you down the stream, some of them will happen to flow with you in sync, but some day you have to let them go. This is the main reason I put together this book (even though it only came to my mind after putting together the rest of the book); to capture the fleeting inspirations and sentiments from the many souls who have touched my life.

Each chapter in this book brings together two seemingly opposite ideas. But I leave the verdict to you, dear reader, whether the poem talks of either one, or maybe both ends of the spectrum…

CONTENTS

I. Lust and Love..1

II. Pain and Healing 17

III. Youth and Growth 35

IV. Finding and Belonging 48

V. Segregate and Connect......................................64

VI. Roots and Freedom 82

I. Lust and Love

Early hours of the morning
Blurred line between light and darkness
In the distant horizon
And within us

- Balcony thoughts, 7 March 2021

Lust and Love

Amateur('s) poem on love

Some seek it to be happy
Some wait and take it easy
Some chase for it but don't have a clue
Whether they should play by the rule

Like a gentle gust of wind
It comes and go without a trace
Or a bolt of blinding lightning
That makes all our hearts race

Some say it's hard to be found
But they just throw it around
They catch it but never hold on
Like a horse unleashed it is gone

As for me, no matter how I try
It never treated me kind, heavens above!
There were times when I wonder why
I wrote this poem about love!

Lust and Love

The Sun and the Sea

Dawn; the sun breaks through the horizon
The sea lights up beneath in one swift movement
The stars it carries sparkle oh what a sight
The sun's the reason it survives the tempestuous night

The sea reaches out to the brilliant beam
But every time it gets close it turns to steam
Sometimes at night I hear it heaves a big sigh
Swaying the boats so vigorously the young birds cry

There was a day, the sun never rose
The sea kept on waiting, the moon above glows
It never noticed, despite the rays the sun shares
It never needs the sea; it has always just been there

The sea never gave up till its waters were frozen
It has no heart but somehow it is broken
With all the burning torches the sun has
It never again penetrated the sea's stony depths

Lust and Love

Dating app

They will come
and only want
the shape of you
the idea of you
how you make them laugh
give them light when it's dark
make up for what they lack
with no strings attached

What can you say though
You do it this way too
It's such a plight
That is just life

Lust and Love

February

You wake up, and suddenly, it's February
Happy día de St. Valentine
You are one of my kind

Lust and Love

Long distance

When you meet someone who likes their toasts soggy like you do
Things seem to fall into place without planning through
Hours will melt into days and into a full moon
And we'll be in the same time zone again soon
. . .
We should be good at this
But it's so hard every time
Maybe one day we'll bridge the distance
And there'll be no need to say goodbye

Lust and Love

Red Ferrari

Wake up feeling frantic
Forgot it's a day off in the week
Prepare for work in a panic
Then realising with relief

That's how it is with you
Still getting used to the idea
Of being not one but two
Ever since you've been here

Wonder where this serenity is placed
Seconds before your name resurface
The thought of you, it rings a bell
And it calms me like a spell

The days go round and round
Monday and its brothers beat you down
Five hectic chorus without an interlude
That you have to be tough regardless of mood

But now riding in the red taxi
Feels like I'm in a Ferrari
For I finally get to come home
To the one I call my own

Lust and Love

Throwback thoughts

Today I saw you in the crowd talking
The smile on your face, like lavender fields blooming
The colours of the rainbow dim in comparison
Suddenly it occurred to me without any reason

I remember back in kindergarten
My best friend was with another having fun
A flame rose in me like a raging war
But I was small I didn't know what it's called

And I know I get jealous easily
I want to be the one who makes you happy
Sometimes it scares me how possessive I can be
I don't really know what I want for me

But we are no more kids with a new found toy
Once you pledge to always be their companion
You know he will be the only boy
No matter how many others catch your attention

Pass the surprising encounters the fluttering of heart
It comes to the most important part
Pass the endless nights writing verses that rhyme
There're more to be promised besides your free time

He may be funny and say words that are pleasing
Or recite the periodic table from the end to beginning
He might have eyes that are sapphire blue
But all those mean nothing 'cause he can never be you

Lust and Love

The one

Maybe you have found "the one"
Or you are finally too tired to run
Who will ever know, but now that we're here
Does it even really matter?

Truth is, I don't feel each week dragging by anymore
Also, there is this wonderful person I adore
Who speaks my mind and has so much more in store

Lust and Love

Autumn

He says he still can't gather his thoughts
Around the fact that we're together
I say it's so amazing that he's got
A way of seeing me as someone better

I did not write this today
To say the above, 'cause you already know
I wrote this for you to say
How disappointed I was some days ago

Disappointed that you still don't see
That I decided not to look back again
The day I said how much you mean to me
When you came with your umbrella in the rain

Don't you ever see
I don't really need someone to lift me
But a pair of hands that is always there
To hold me and wipe away my tears

Looking at the world through an open door
Seems like I am already free
I don't remember how it felt anymore
When the night closes in around me

And I know sometimes it's not easy
Like latching on to the winds

Lust and Love

So thank you for bearing with me
Through my bitter and crazy times

Life has taught me so far
How everyone has their own story
And though you have your own scars
They match mine perfectly

Lust and Love

The hotel

Naked bodies
Do no magic for me
Tell me your story
How you feel about
The smell of clean linens
Sunlight spilling over the curtains
The sound of slamming doors
Early morning goers down the hall
And above all, if the taste of me
Makes you forget, if just briefly -
That we are all inherently lonely

Lust and Love

April

You wake up, things are different but the same
Out of habit, you play the tunes that got you going
And realised, they are no longer consoling
In fact, you dimly register the alarm buzzing
Over the sound of your spirits soaring

It's like all along
We've been waiting
For things to fall in place
Like the way they do now
Isn't it amazing how
It can happen just in days?

Lust and Love

Dusk till dawn

It's one of the worst feelings
In bed staring at the ceiling
Silhouettes often give the illusion
You're in both the past and present

When you walk on tightrope
Will love suffice to cope?
Is it all up to chance
to sustain a romance?

Have to stop overthinking
Why are the tears flowing?
Whatever happens is for the best
Things will look up after you rest

Sun rays seeped through the curtains
Through the patches of my mind
It always finds a way, even when it rains
It only takes a little time

And you're here with me for another morning
It's one of the best feelings

Memorandum

This place was a mere checkpoint
Temporary stop for a wanderer
It was you who showed me its colours
Where I hadn't noticed in years

Laughing with a beer on the roof
Away from all the chaos
City lights across the harbour
Night owls working past the hours
Making to the hilltop in the rain
Squinting at boats in the horizon
Flitting between alleys at dawn
Before the flower market open
When hawkers prepare their stalls
Next to freshly printed newspapers

Guess I just realised one day
You were a mere checkpoint too
But even if I had known another way
I wouldn't have done anything new

Lust and Love

Archives

There's a tiny book
I keep on a shelf
Inconspicuous with just one look
Among everything else

Written in it are memories of faces
Our paths crossed in various places

You may ask why it doesn't have your name
As we sit side by side one winter's night
Because with you it doesn't feel the same
It's like coming home at last on a flight

And we'll be laughing as we read and go through
All the wrongs it took for me to meet you

.

II. Pain and Healing

But how I wish I could have the nerves again
To dream and give so selflessly, though I know how it'll end!

- Diary entry, 15 October 2009

Pain and Healing

The first boy

There's a lot going on tonight across the street
Music booming makes the whole place shake
Being just half the reason I'm not asleep
My own thoughts were enough to keep me awake

That hand locked with yours, it could have been mine
Though I know to her I can never compare
I've forgotten how to not pretend to be fine
My hopes and wishes turned into my worst nightmare

And they're singing about undying love
In this familiar melody
Moonlit strolls, counting stars above,
Serenades on guitars; things never meant for me

Maybe I should go to the extreme
Among the disco lights I would find a lover
Things are never really what they seem
Love doesn't take me seriously; why should I vice versa?

Pain and Healing

Eulogy (for an unreciprocated love)

It's so hard to say goodbye
When I know there won't be a next time

It hurts to think of yesterday
When I thought we had forever
The flowers in May
The snow in Winter

It's confusing about the future
Now I'm convinced it's over
The autumn leaves, the sky painted blue
Will never be as wonderful as you

Pain and Healing

Closing curtains

All the world's a stage, us in an amphitheatre
And Life the playwright with its dark sense of humour

I know for every decision it's hard not to sway
And wonder what would happen the other way

But if a person like me can still be entitled to wishes
Just as there's a place where the lost wanderer confesses
I wish this is the last time I hurt you again
I wish that I could understand
Why things couldn't stay the same
When I was ready to give up my name

And I wish I could hear what you're saying now
The sound of the audience is getting too loud
Maybe in time we'll find our voices and heal
Until then I'm sorry. Goodbye, and thank you.

Pain and Healing

Karma

It'll be another sleepless night
Another bird that took flight
A change of heart requires no reason
Looks like a taste of your own medicine
Maybe you should stop opening the door
"I will just never love anymore."
Probably it's the anaesthetic you took
'Cause you smiled at your own joke
At all the times you've said it before.

Pain and Healing

Suffocating

Every time. You think at last someone understands
Then life always has other plans
There's no way out that you can find
'Cause it hurts like suffocating. Every time.

Pain and Healing

The path not taken

We sat on the sofa, side by side together
We laughed about something and I held you tighter
A thought occurred to me - even then I knew better
That this is a dream and we've not spoken in forever
Funny how this sense in my arms seem real
Though I've never known the way it feels

Remember how we stood watching the sky painted red
All was silent but my thoughts were soundlessly weaving
A story for the two of us months and years ahead
It's the downside of a brain that never stops whirling

But a heart does get weary
Burning with desire for too long
Without anything to feed it
Without a tune for its song

And the heart can get heavy
Passing by places never visited
Weighed down by the memory
That was never created

I can say I still miss you
But that's not entirely true
You were the adventure I chose not to set foot in
It's normal to glorify what could have been
Once I'm back on my feet and the moment's passed
You're just a fleeting sentiment that did not last.

Pain and Healing

Thank you

"Those were the best days of my life," you once said to me.

I also used to mourn for the "good old days"
Thinking there will be no replacement
But life went on, I made new memories
That restored my optimism

Then I met you. And I wish you knew
Those were the best days of my life too

And I hope someday we can say
Looking back at our time together
Those were the best days of our life
But they were not the last ever.

Pain and Healing

Part of me

I am just thinking
of things I thought I will remember
of people who seemed will stay forever

I used to have time then and there
To weave them into words on paper
But what more can I do
I have exhausted my vocabulary
and pool of tears for you
Ever since that day, you see
Time seems to have held its breath
It has been so long since I have felt
The surging feeling only words can bring
Resonating with the Broca's area of your brain

Maybe I was somehow drained
My wishes lost in life's cruel tease
But still, I couldn't contain
My glee to have finished this little piece

It's a part of me I still recognize
What a relief it is to know
And I secretly promise
This time I'll never let her go

Pain and Healing

Live again

Take time to process the pain
Face your demon, turn it into a friend
You will learn to love life again.

Pain and Healing

Relapse

I feel like a wrecking cyclone
A trail of bodies behind me
But I need another distraction
Amid the stormy sea

So done with finding someone
To accept the whirlpool I am
That has never worked out
A myriad of reasons I guess
Maybe it'll always be in chaos
Maybe it's happier on the shallows

Why figure it out instead
When nothing really matters
"I just really hope," I said,
"that I don't harm another."
But my dear friend she said
"And not yourself either."

Pain and Healing

Epiphany

Sometimes it hits me
I admit with pangs of envy
Seeing pictures of smiling faces
Held in each other's embraces
They seem to have it figured out
But then it struck me
That it's just a cut-out
Of a moment in their story
Their happiness
And my flash of envy
Are just isolated notes
In an unfinished symphony

Pain and Healing

Reunion

But as the shadow drew nearer
As the familiar face became clear
I felt none of the pain I was bracing for
Nor any of the desire I was dreading
There it was, somebody I used to know
Like a book that once filled my evenings
But maybe it's the book
Or remembering the cost it took
I've lost the thirst to go on reading

Pain and Healing

Dear ex-lover

How long has it been?
Spring was just here
When she made her exit
Can't imagine how
This time last year
You thought this time you'd make it
Keep replaying those scenes
You never know what it means
You'll resort to a long drink
As it hurts too much to think
But you'll wake up one day
and decide it can't go on this way…

Sorry, I just know, it's what I would do
To deal with the pain that I put you through

Pain and Healing

For a friend

It takes courage
to go after what you desire
Yet even more courage to let go
when it's no longer what you want

Pain and Healing

Miracle

Something wonderful
Will come out of those tears
Sometimes though
It can take up to years

I know it's hard to see
When your vision is blurred
So far out at sea
The silver linings obscured

It's alright though
That's why I am here
To remind you your miracle
Will one day appear

Pain and Healing

The poison

Some moments swell
Into a veil
Lingering to last
Long after they've passed

A blank period in time
As if I was drunk on the memory
I guess I had been happy
That was before you left me

There are times though
I wear the darkness like a shroud
Coz it's a familiar friend
And at least I know

The same pain won't get worse
And if it gets too heavy
I can always write out the ink-blackness
Before it tries to consume me

Wounds

Dear gentle soul
You don't have to tie to their wounds
as if they were your own
Everyone is doing their best
but some may hurt you in the process
The truth is, it's suffocating
When you're doing your own healing
So before dishing out your empathy
Make sure you leave yourself plenty

III. Youth and Growth

May thy eternal summer never fade.

- Instagram caption, 13 July 2021

Youth and Growth

For me, from me (2009)

Not long ago, you longed to be a famous person
Someone that creates inspiration
Someone so influential
She could set an example

At school, there were lab experiments
We dwelt deep and had so-call 'achievements'
Though numerous books piled our shelves
We never really understood ourselves

Then you met someone you thought you knew
They painted all your dreams anew
But they soon left as if they never were
Sealing their paths for another wanderer

There were stone hedges you thought you could count on
To these you clung on gratefully
They all looked so tough and strong
Who knew they were caving in internally?

Why are you so faithful, in short naive?
What makes you have in people so much believe?
The millions of masks they had created
To hide their faces, making it so complicated

Maybe you've stopped trying to understand
We are all but like specks of sand
Remember yourself in spite of things they've done
Then you have already won

Youth and Growth

A-level study break

The sun hangs shining in the morning air
As I stroll along the silent corridor
Familiar sounds of the school bell at noon
Across the playground, the sweet flowerbed blooms
The brown tiles that line the stairs, so well I have known;
Every classroom on every floor, a seat I called my own

At the gate a janitor lady stops me
"Which class should you be in?"
Wonder if she'll take me seriously
If I say I'm older than sixteen

The trees seem to wave and smile
As if they somehow know
Let me stay here for a while
I'm in no hurry to go

Youth and Growth

Psychology major

Growing up feels like waking in a bustling city
A pull from the realm of fantasy
To the brutal truth of reality

I came here to learn what makes me this way
But they told me my behaviours everyday
Might be interwoven by genes too small to see
And millions other can share the same gene with me

Just maybe, I am not special at all
So I should go on searching no more
For I thought there were rainbows waiting for me
But no, they're just optical illusions I see

The moon shines among the clouds, a glowing drop of silver
Such moving tales and ballads it once inspired!
But a shiny slap of rock, that's all it'll ever be
What more could it be without someone here with me?

Guitar chords fill the air in the silent silvery beams
They tug at your heart seams, like fragments of broken dreams
But there's no need to fear, for as the dawn breaks
The sun will chase way the chill and mend the heartaches

Then I realised no one's special as we are all unique
Different are our purposes and paths we choose to seek
Everyone's in this battle, there's no time to be weak

Youth and Growth

Dear self (2018)

Dear self a year from now,
Have you gotten it figured out? Are you better at it somehow?
Are the nights still excruciatingly painful
Occasionally when you walk alone?
Has your heart grown big enough
To take another person's burden
Even when you can barely speak
Feeling the weight of your own?
Have your ambitions expired
Are you finally putting yourself first?
Have you been too tired of feeling tired
Too drained to put feelings into words?
On such days when I don't have a clue
I shut out the world and think of you
'Cause you know me and everything I go through
And won't judge no matter what I do

You'll look back on me as a memory
And though I know it's not the best
I hope you'll still recall it fondly
I hope you don't love yourself less

Youth and Growth

Uni mates

In my dream we were gathered round
A version of us from an older time
Talking wildly, laughter in the background
And everything was going to be fine

Sometimes I feel we grew up too fast
Caught in the whirlpool before learning to swim
They see your efforts only when you win
And we reach out for stimulation
To numb the sensation
Of a million turmoils in our hearts

You're rushing through the day
Hardly enough time for thinking
But it shouldn't be this way
Living it all without feeling

Because we've got each other
In this massive whirlpool
And we can hold on together
To make the world a little less cruel

Youth and Growth

Unfinished

Tidying the stash at a corner of my room
Scraps of paper fell out from where they loom

Bits of sentences and phrases
Almost like a mindless doodle
The handwriting of someone else;
It was mine, some time ago

Wonder if life had always been this way
Incomplete verses left for another day
Half-formed ideas with thoughts astray
Interests and passion that didn't stay

Have you ever wondered
If it would be better
To grab a blank piece of paper
And just start all over?

But in fact you know
You don't have to hide the scrawls
For what make a story beautiful
Are the unfinished explores

Youth and Growth

7th June

Twenty-some years ago, on a night like this one
Thunder and rain; the sky had come undone
I was born the morning after, that's what they say
A new week in June, on a sunny Monday

Somehow that used to make me feel special
Maybe I could make the storms come and go
Turns out the storms were inside me all along
Sometimes dormant, sometimes beautifully strong

People are like storm clouds too
Guess I eventually came to know
Some bring a lesson as they come to you
But give you the biggest one when they go

Life is often about having strength
To accept the only thing constant is change
In a way, those who left are still with you together
A life-long journey, to carry our own weather

Youth and Growth

Time after time

Maybe this is part of growing up
Knowing that life goes on
But part of you will still hold on
Pretending that memories will suffice
As reality tears at the seams
Day after day, you compromise
Some dreams will do to stay as dreams

Yet this is part of growing up too:
Learning that you don't need closure
As time is the great teacher who
Will make us forget to remember

Still eventually we reminisce
And know nothing will take their place
But words can lay most feelings to rest
And in time you will see
You're not as undeserving of happiness
As you make yourself out to be

Youth and Growth

Interval

Maybe I just need a break
From being strong for too long
Maybe it's too much to take
Or something about me is just wrong

I squeezed my eyes shut and kept my head low
But just couldn't stop the flow
Of thoughts creeping into consciousness
Constantly reminding, that I am a mess

Perhaps the best way out of this cruelty
Is through headphones plugged in to a familiar tune
Don't bother at this rate to go looking for me
For you may find me engrossed in memory
From a time when life seemed to be easy
But this is just an illusion through a cocoon

There had always been problems
Life has never been a garden of Eden
But I started remembering the younger me
How things she dreaded eventually came to pass
Though I'm not exactly the person she hoped to be
In one way or other, things turned out fine at last

So now with my heart still beating
I refuse to surrender
Until I make myself remember
I've got to go on fighting

Youth and Growth

Dear self (2019)

Looks like we are here again
Attempting to gather yourself but in vain
Maybe you're trying to be something you're not
Truth is, you never had much time to give it a thought

Must be tiring, look how far you've ventured
Maybe these roads aren't needing what you offer
At times I think you push yourself too much
Whatever they may think, you've tried hard enough

Dear self a year ago
It's not a sin to go with the flow
I have seen and felt as you did
Don't settle for less than splendid

-- In response to "Dear self (2018)"

Youth and Growth

Reminisce

Ah, I was only twenty
A few months was like eternity
And the whole world seemed to be
Within the confines of this university

Youth and Growth

Alma mater

This place next time around
Wonder how it'll be?
I won't be the same person
And there won't be the same tree

IV. Finding and Belonging

Everything's just not what they seem
There are faults we can never redeem
So I came to accept the splendours of the rain
Finding the peace I had searched for in vain

- Rainy day thoughts, 10 September 2009

Finding and Belonging

Scenes from childhood home

The sound of the guitar breaks through the stillness
Like waves rippling across the lagoon
Here I sit here feeling aimless
Another hot Saturday afternoon

Remember gazing at the starry skies at night
Everything was going alright
The occasional cry of the mockingbirds
Gave me a calmness beyond any words

Remember the breeze, how it had swept
All the worries and secrets I had kept
The sunlight overhead so bright
Like the smiles on people's faces in sight

The sound of the guitar echoes through my mind
Someday, somewhere I will find
The place that I truly belong
And my heart will be filled with its song

Finding and Belonging

Memory of February

You had a real shot at happiness
Loneliness makes the best veil
The past looks like cherry blossoms
As the present becomes stale

Everyone wants somebody
To somehow fix the trauma
But getting far too weary
To go through all the drama

And it's no surprise
As you prop up in bed
Dry your red puffy eyes
Hungover from the dread

Trying not to let down your guard
Maybe it's the wrong place you're looking
But how do you know where to start
When you don't know what you're missing?

Finding and Belonging

Christmas

The bare trees stood anticipating in unison
A chill lingers; as if time's momentarily frozen
The sky opened, out of the fissure they wade
Delicate ice crystals, like the wishes children made

For all the poets this is an inspiration they won't miss
Night wind swirls the snowflakes into a dazzling bliss
If Shakespeare had seen this he would not say
Shall I compare thee to a summer's day?

A flake flutters onto my glove with its crystalline structure
Pure like the white rose, much more rare than its red sister
Every pattern's unique; there's not a single copy
Out of millions of them I'm glad that one had stayed for me

Not till next morning when the melted snow vaporize
Will I remember they could never be around for long
But for this moment of joy I am willing to pay the price
Let me stay in this illusion where I think I belong

Finding and Belonging

Brain damage

It's an old diary that I'm reading alone
No wonder they talk of it in such foreboding tone
Every entry is a tragedy of its own
A girl whose emotions could not find their way home

Desperately seeking a trace of evidence
That her presence on this world is significant
Some tried to approach but she waved them away
Not forgetting the humiliation that particular day

Time seems to flow slower for a person
When you don't know where you belong
Her heart's straining to leap out of the prison
She's been building for so long

Now people are coming in with a cake - "Happy Birthday Tammy!"

Flipping over to the front of the diary
I was shocked to find the owner was me
But I hope things will be different, after this special day
And all those things in the past, might as well go away

Finding and Belonging

Vacation

Some people travel when their hearts get too laden
To escape to where there's no one else
But in the end, you realise in a sudden
There's only coming to terms with yourself

Finding and Belonging

Typhoon signal

On an oddly calm morning
Alone on the street walking
Going along with the people
Pretending I knew where to go

I have no problem to wander
All this time is not squandered
Idleness is when beauty is born
Especially amidst the storm.

Finding and Belonging

Sober thoughts

When you've come a long way
And have been running for so long
Is it a tragedy to realise today
The track you started at was wrong?

Sometimes when their voices are too loud
I forget why I'm here in the first place
Just another face merging with the crowd
Complying with the rest for nobody's sake

At night I toss and turn with thoughts
Though by day it's easy to laugh at them
Crying is for those who are lost;
I don't want you to think I am

I could turn to what I used to do
Find myself again among the pages
But words seem to forsake me too
Out of reach, hidden in cages

For I used to have the honour of being their friend
No need for me to borrow from lyrics then
It felt like a shopaholic seeing a sale
Like a child receiving a post by mail

Finding and Belonging

And it seemed like I was in control
But now, how I feel I don't even know
Do I still embrace the passion
Or is it for sheer attention?

Truth be told, I'm just another girl
Navigating this kaleidoscopic world
Despite the odds, I'm still searching for perfection
And this might be my path to self-destruction

Finding and Belonging

Nine lives

Feline predator
Ferocious like your ancestor
Ready to prance at the aperture
Where the intruder hovers

Your curiosity is never curbed
Most things beyond your comprehension
Somehow you sleep undisturbed
By any pangs of frustration

Do those wide, innocent eyes
Tell where your loyalty lies?
Are you just seeking the next victim
Someone to do your bidding?

Or are you looking for something
Beyond this safe haven
Where troubles seem to be at bay
But night turns uneventfully into day?

Finding and Belonging

Nomad

It's your choice in a sense
You cannot possibly
Enjoy the liberty of walking free
But scorn the occasional loneliness

Finding and Belonging

Workday morning

It's so cold that your fingers
Protest as you ran the tap water
Don't pull away, it's just a feeling
Got to go on, though it's piercing

You've been accelerating so fast
Thought you were indestructible and all
Wasn't long before you realise
There was really nothing to break the fall

But seems like you're getting better
Playing by the script with more vigour
So glad to see how much you grow
Riding the highs and bearing with the lows

Don't be afraid; for nothing is written
Raise your voice; and people will listen
When all else fails and everything hurts
Among these pages you'll find your words

Finding and Belonging

Villain

All this show and drama
Hurling yourself through fire
Breaking into pieces all over
Holding yourself back together

Just to find someone who understands
Like home to a lost deer
Someone who holds your hands
And say "You belong here."

That's why you bent over backwards
For the scraps of love you thought you deserve
Made leave every time before the pain could sink in
They called you a villain, yet you were your own victim.

Till one day you realised
And it was a relief that brought tears
As you stopped running and dropped your disguise
And told yourself - "You belong here."

Finding and Belonging

Beyond the room

These walls are impeccably white
Yet absurdly thin
How frustrating it is
For these voices to seep in

"You'll never make it out of here"
"No matter what, you can't be heard"
The words reverberate off the ceiling
The turmoils inside you stirring

Maybe you're not scared
Of the voices out there
Maybe you fear that they are wrong;
And there's somewhere out there you belong

Or worse, you fear that the voices aren't real
That the one making you settle for less
Stowed in the comforts of your confinement
Has been yourself and no one else

Finding and Belonging

Fresh leaf

Soon it will be a distant memory
All the self-doubt, feelings of inadequacy

I have no way of knowing
About the place I am going
Whether I will still find
Things I try to leave behind

But the sun is golden when I woke
And in its blazing rays I soaked
A chapter in my book is done
And a new day has just begun

Finding and Belonging

Greatest party

The world's a big party in progress
If you see it from a different view
While you're busy entertaining the guests
Don't forget to celebrate you

V. Segregate and Connect

Serendipity nowadays might as well have been a mere social media algorithm.

- Instagram caption, 30 November 2020

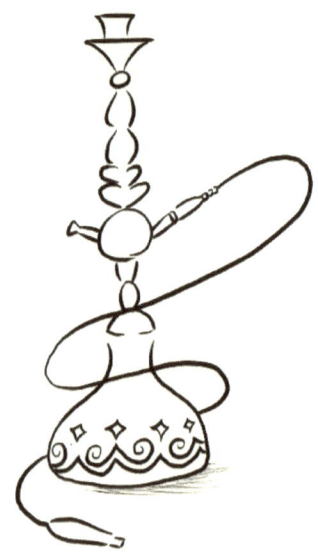

Segregate and Connect

Balcony thoughts

It's just you alone
Just you and your tears
No one will know
No one ever has to bear
The heaviness of this sight
On top of their own fight

Segregate and Connect

Unbearable lightness

Sleep, blessed sleep in the evening
Turning on your side feels like a chore
Slow down, you're not missing anything
Being human is enough daring
You deserve a trophy and so much more
For bearing with the sheer weight of living

Segregate and Connect

1st January

The night is young but there are plenty at the bar
Yet more flocking in after birth of the new year
The crowd is wild but there's something there
Hanging on every glass and silverware

You understand all too well I bet
People seeking connection or to forget
Filling their cups and, hopefully the emptiness
That only comes when night brings darkness

And you suddenly feel in sync
As if you've met them before
You shuffled with the bass and don't think
Of life's many hassles no more

Why do you need alcohol to speak your mind?
Or show you how to have a good time?
If you are ever cold or lonely
It only proves you can still feel
I hope in time that you will see
It's not something you need to heal

You know it's not easy to live
But you've been a survivor so far
That's the most important thing I believe
You should be celebrating at the bar

Pandemic

I like watching the pouring rain
There's comfort in the chaos
It's one thing that stayed the same
From the world we used to know

These days leave us no room
So we have to make our own
Though none of us got the answer
At least we are better together

Segregate and Connect

Quarantine

Leaving the house for the first time in days
The doctor scribbled as I described my case

It's always when the darkness comes
When you realise you had an easy run
Though it seemed like the worst for so long
But naturally, life proves you wrong

I can't stop longing again, the fantasy
Where our lives were not under such scrutiny
When we did not have to fight for dignity

How is this fair? But was it ever?
You know you never took it for granted
But any shred of warmth seems not enough
Whenever the darkness engulfs

Look at the plans they made indeed
When tomorrow is not guaranteed
When I cannot even comprehend
How this poem will end

Life must go on evolving
That is what matters
To change what will happen
Or how it is remembered

Segregate and Connect

Can't tell if it'll ever get better
But this much I can fathom
The flame in us burns brighter
Whenever the darkness comes

Segregate and Connect

In between

There's a kind of addiction
Staring off into space
The words just won't come
For a feeling I can't place

It's not that complicated
Yet you can't complain about it
Like a mild itch or thirst
But you know you've had worse

They say life has ups and downs
But few talks of the in-between
Mindless and mediocre moments
Days deprived of adrenaline

It's when you dig out old photos
Borrow stories from tv episodes
Cry for someone who isn't real
Just to relive how it felt to feel

Maybe you do crave the drama
Maybe in some ways
Getting yourself out of order
Is just what you need on some days

Dying of the light

I am in a dark place
and I should have known
Been running at a brisk pace
Now it hunts me down

It tells me give it a rest
'Cause it's all meaningless

There's nothing to find
Being part of something bigger
Life will be unkind
People corrupted by power
Nothing really matters
So just don't bother

I heard it out
What if it's right?
I always thought it was about
Touching another life

But have I done more damage
Than good with my advantage?
Trying to fulfil a purpose
That I don't recognize

What if all this labour
Is merely seeking approval
Preying on people who favour
Something to sympathize with?

Segregate and Connect

Maybe someday I would sink
In that happy oblivion again
Forget to think
As I fill up my brain
With little goals and schemes
The stuff of passionate dreams

I'll be back on the race
And it will be okay
I'll be back at my happy place
But just not today

Segregate and Connect

Residual blues

What are we living for
Just waiting for the next tide
Anything to take our mind off
The absurdity of this ride

Segregate and Connect

The black filter

It's all so sudden
The way it happens
One moment you were having a blast
The next you're wondering how long it can last

Someone once told me they were sure
All things that bring us pleasure
Earthly or spiritual, are merely distractions
From the fact that life is a dreary existence

And demons who haunt us when we're alone
Have always been lurking in the dark zone
Just occasionally drowned out in the crowd
When the laughters are sufficiently loud

But what if life was meant to be lived without a care
Punctuated by moments of self-doubts and despair
Which are merely distractions instead
Shielding us from the broadway ahead

Maybe good times don't have to be stolen
And happiness doesn't require us fighting

And all those times we feel lonely or unworthy
Just support us to inspire another soul in distress
That life has always been rose-tinted naturally
Without the glasses we wear when depressed.

Segregate and Connect

Resignation ponderings

When I was small, I used to ponder
What are we all living for?
Staring up at the distant galaxy
And saw a shooting star gone astray

Down it would fall
A burning meteor
I heard the roaring sound
As it shot towards the ground

And I pled; don't let this be the end of the world
There's still so much life has yet to unfurl
The countless parties and nameless faces that await
As long as I live, there'll be something to anticipate

And the roaring sound faded
For it had just been a plane
Cutting the night sky like a blade
Blinking past my windowpane

Now I get off the mass transit and slowly trudged home
Above me, a flashing plane tore across the horizon
I think of my younger self pleading with the sky
But this time no words, no thoughts cross my mind

Giving up is easy, as those who hold on knows
The choice is entirely mine, yet I just can't let it go
So the question is not whether I will make it through
But whether the view is worth the struggle that is due

Segregate and Connect

Digital fortress

It's another new day
Staring at the miniature display
Refreshing and scrolling
Alone on your phone
You know it's an illusion but still can't help thinking
Of people leading lives much better than your own
You crave for some sort of activity
To save you from this drudgery
Although the buzzing notifications don't necessarily mean
That a lot of people care where you have been

You've been running away for too long
It's always one thing or another
Ignoring the inevitable void
Putting away emotions till later
When it's safe for them to break free
Where you're sure no one will see
Funny how they are gifts from birth
Yet don't seem to hold much worth
All these demands during daytime hustling
Does not seem to advocate thinking or feeling

I'm only human; that I know clearly
Sometimes my only wish is merely
To get lost in a story other than my own
Till I fall asleep at the brink of dawn

Segregate and Connect

Perhaps we seek brief moments of connection
To make up for those passed in confusion
From the uneasiness of wearing a skin
That we don't really seem to fit in

Clinging onto hope that when the pieces meet
We will feel in the end it was all worth it

Segregate and Connect

REM

The small hours of the night before drifting off to sleep
The first few blurry seconds in the morning
Are the moments you're most vulnerable to feeling
Sentiments you thought you no longer keep

But I know as the day goes on I'll be better
Because I can carry my own weather
Celebrate the sunshine and dance in the rain
Love myself for feeling awesome and feeling pain

Segregate and Connect

Onepiece

Stay with this feeling. Don't bury or ignore it.
Do you know where this is going? How long can you stand this?
I want so much to live, feel all the energy it brings
But there's never enough time to do all the things
Or is it a matter of time? Because at times like now
I'm slump in front of the laptop watching online streams
Of coloured cartoon characters that found their way somehow
To interesting adventures and fighting for their dreams
And I'm addicted as I scroll through the episodes to view
As if watching them can numb this emptiness I feel
This sense of craving for something I can't name
The desire for living everyday not the same
Can one be helped if one doesn't know what's wrong?
Is it normal to not know for what it is that I long?

Purgatory

Add pasta while stirring
Heat the mix till tender
There's something missing
I can't string these words together

Warm rays of sun in lazy Spring
Earthy whiff of grass after the rain
Somehow I am feeling
Like losing a part of who I am

And this may be the writer's curse
To either harbour an unquenched thirst
Morbid with regret and pain
Chasing shadows in vain

Or to be fortunate at long last
No longer haunted by memories of the past
To live blissfully free from desires
But secretly yearns for the melancholy that inspires

VI. Roots and Freedom

Freedom is a myth. You will never be free unless you are completely alone.

- Shower thoughts, 27 March 2020

Roots and Freedom

After work

I get home and greeted the familiar sights
From the kitchen, aromatic fumes and lights
I find myself thinking maybe it's not all bad
But some days it's hell and I do feel bad

And I had to keep reminding myself
To loosen my grip on the hilt
That I am just like everyone else
And I shouldn't be loaded with guilt
For dining out more than one night a week
For messaging too long before sleep
For having an idea what I want to be happy
For keeping the things he bought me
For the urge to break out from this territory
For the desire to be free

Freedom, that which is so often sought-after
I never thought I would lose it to my life-giver
Tell me I do not have to listen
When they said I am a disgrace
For tearing my family apart
Just because I follow my heart
Tell me it is not a crime
That this saddle is mine to mount
'Cause this life is a gift but now it's time
For me to live it the way I want

Masquerade

Yet another endless lecture
From the other side of the door
You have had enough
They claim they do it out of love

You thought of washing it down with alcohol
But know better than that take
Doesn't it just mark you as immature
The point they are trying to make?

You keep sane, you reason
You become a better person
Than you ever cared to be in the past
You try so hard to show
Only you can be in control
Every day, it's like putting on a mask

They still expect you to smile
They don't see you up at night
When you crumple into a pile
What does life want from you, right?

Sometimes you even doubt
Maybe it's you after all
Who can't see what it's all about
Oblivious to your downfall

Roots and Freedom

But you're set on what you choose
I know you are that kind of girl
Maybe it's fatal like a noose;
But you'll never turn back for the world

Life feels like a roller coaster ride
Sometimes you don't really get to steer
But why would you have to hide
Rather than roll with the highs and the fear?

Know this; you do deserve better
So don't give in, don't sink further
Take your life back off the shelf
If not for anyone, at least for yourself

Hongkonger in 2020

Should I go or should I stay?
I know we live in a time where
Things get more absurd every day
Whatever I do here or there

I should be grateful to still have choices
In a place with disappearing voices
The city has long been sick and coughing
Before they put the last nail in the coffin

Though it's no longer possible
For things to be how they used to be
There had been passionate people
There had been good memories

The "Pearl of the Orient"
Has long lost its glory
But don't let it be forgotten
A mere footnote in history
Go on our obscure journey
And help pass on the story

Roots and Freedom

Brave New World

Behind joy, always the silent acknowledgement
That it's more than just a simple sentiment
Streets are cleared, but are not forgotten
Despite their claims of what never happened

Ain't it a shame. Like a burning flame
Stability is apparently built on turmoils
And so often you don't have a choice
Who live with the guilt or who sacrifice

Thoughts on Lantau Peak

I say at near twenty-eight
There may be things I should do
Before it's too late

But for this place it seems
Any plan has lost its meaning
Except those schemes
That involve leaving

Blame it on the times
But as life goes on you find
They were never here to serve you
It's all about what you do

Come what may
Be ready to play
The cards on your way
That's how we've come all the way

Roots and Freedom

Prison of freedom

You crave for freedom
Yet seek it in vain
The idea brings obsession
that only leads to pain

Slave of your impulses
Your heart out on your sleeves
Won't you come to your senses
Come home this Christmas eve?

Roots and Freedom

9600 km

Nine thousand six hundred kilometres
From the place that I called home
Where the city lights kept their glamours
But the familiarity is gone

Bustling crowds during rush hour
Are a sight no more now
Empty stores, empty aisles
No students at wooden tables

Except for queues snaking their way
Into former community centres
Bedsheets and linens in the chilling rain
Like white flags in surrender
For the values, the identity
That we held so dear
Along with the version of our history
We once thought was clear

On the other side of the continent
A more brutal war is waging
I know I may never comprehend
Those people's suffering

But I have not forgotten
The rallying cry of might

Roots and Freedom

The black parade in unison
Under a weaving chain of lights

All the people defending their home
Share a similar dream
That someday their soil will return
To its glory and gleam

And it's my sole comfort to know
We're different yet so much the same
Nine thousand six hundred kilometres away
A piece of my home lives on in me

Atmosphere

Rocket man
How lonely it must feel
To leave everything familiar
Break out of your atmosphere

On this particular night
With the distant stars so bright
You can't help but wonder
If the home you miss is still there;

You thought of people
That seem lightyears away
Maybe another orbit
Will bring you with them again

One more revolution
Of the Earth around the sun
You'll always remember them
Though the days are forever gone

Life is a journey
Of moving on and letting go
Everything is temporary
Ain't it both sad and wonderful?

ABOUT THE AUTHOR

Tammy was born and raised in Hong Kong. She discovered her flair for poetry in school when writing a love poem for an English literature assignment. Her fascination with human emotions and behaviours inspired her to complete a Bachelor of Psychology. Writing has always been her means to string together wandering thoughts, and through her words she hopes to liberate other gentle souls.

In recent years, the unfolding of events in Hong Kong led her to re-examine her cultural roots. Many of her poems draw inspiration from her own and others' stories, exploring universal topics of self-identity, healing, life transitions, and the desire to belong. Tammy currently lives in Manchester, United Kingdom and enjoys the diverse and vibrant community.

Follow her work on Instagram @wordsintheflow

How was your experience reading Words in the Flow? Did any part resonate with you? I'd love to hear about it.

Your honest review will mean a lot to me!

Scan the QR code below to leave me a review:

Amazon.co.uk

www.ingramcontent.com/pod-product-compliance
Lightning Source LLC
Chambersburg PA
CBHW030454010526
44118CB00011B/932